Instant

ANTHONY FLORES
Elementary Teacher and Art Consultant
Sacramento, California

Fearon Teacher Aids
Carthage, Illinois

Simon & Schuster
Supplementary Education Group

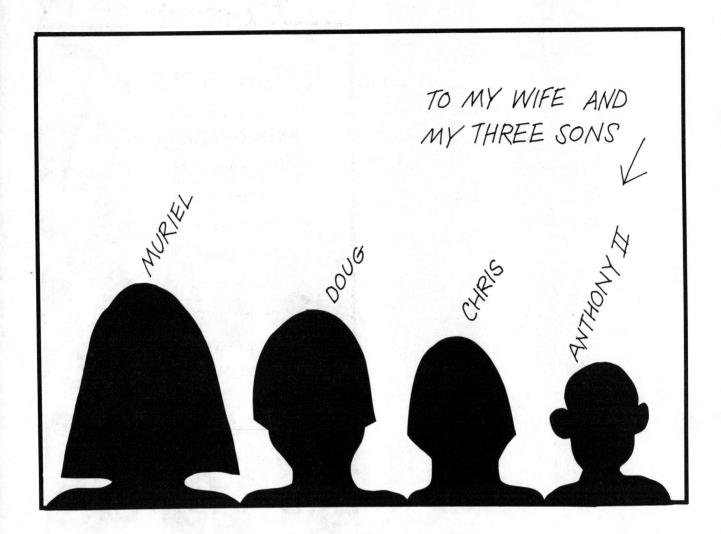

TO MY WIFE AND MY THREE SONS

MURIEL DOUG CHRIS ANTHONY II

Editorial supervision by: Peter Cross
Editing by: Nancy Tune
Cover and interior design by: Jane Mitchell
Border patterns and art by: Anthony Flores

ISBN-0-8224-3899-2
Printed in the United States of America.

Contents

Preface

For a number of years, I have been involved in teacher-training courses in art. One area that I feel is often overlooked is the effectiveness of bulletin boards. An attractive bulletin board will sell itself. It can motivate and even inspire the students, with little effort on the part of the teacher.

This book does not deal with the subject matter of bulletin boards, as there are many sources available in this area. The main objective of this book is to give the teacher samples of borders that can enhance any board in the classroom.

The first section of the book is a general guide to preparing borders. The remaining sections contain the patterns from which borders can be made. These patterns are arranged by theme. First there are general borders—geometric patterns that can be used at any time. Next there are borders for the three seasons of the school year. For each season, general motifs and holidays are represented. In the last section of the book proper may be found special borders on international themes. These borders may be used in connection with social studies, ethnic studies, and special holidays. The Appendix contains selected patterns which have been enlarged to double size. At the beginning of the Appendix you'll find directions for their use.

The patterns in this book are duplicatable and may be varied in a number of ways. Teachers should feel free to experiment with the patterns, adding or deleting cuts to create their own borders.

And now, with scissors in hand, let's begin!

ANTHONY FLORES

Preparing Borders

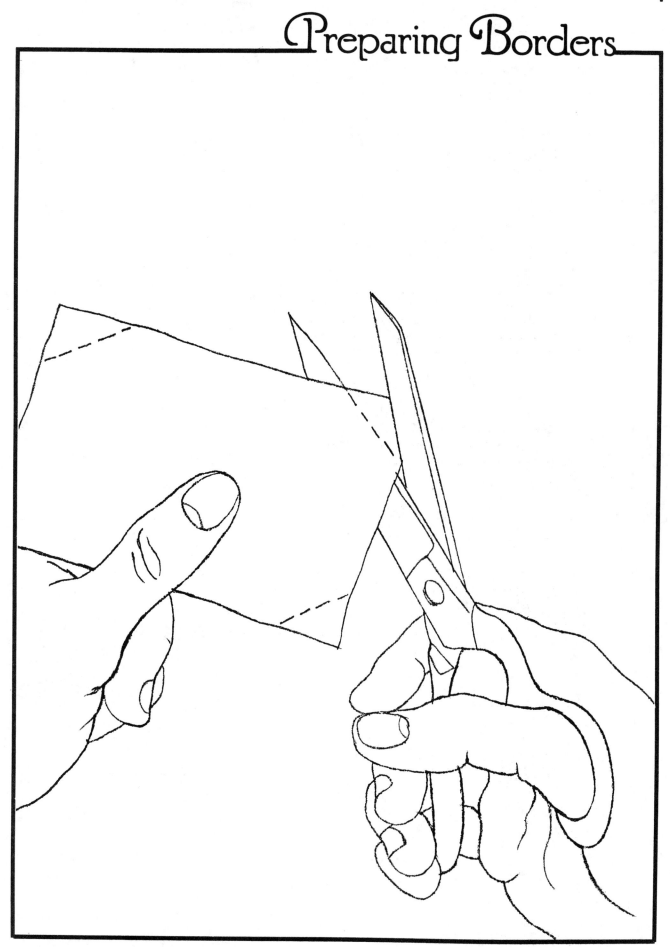

A Step-by-Step Guide
to Preparing Bulletin Board Borders

Step 1

Select a border pattern from this book. You can choose among general geometric patterns, seasonal and holiday patterns, and the international patterns.

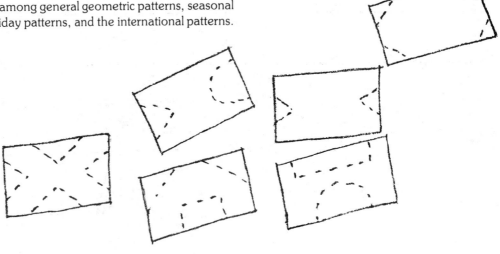

Step 2

Decide on the color you wish to use for your border.

Step 3

Cut strips of construction paper 18 inches by 3 inches. Cut as many strips as necessary to enclose your bulletin board.

Step 4

A. Fold one strip as shown in the diagram below.

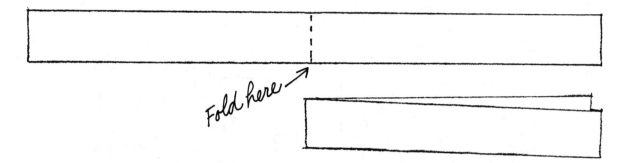

Fold here →

B. Fold the strip in half again.

Fold here ↗

Your folded strip should now look like this.

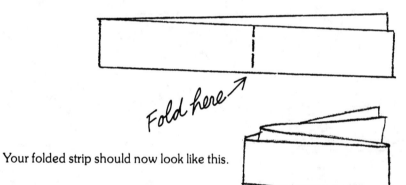

Step 5

Using one of the methods described on pages 4 and 5, cut the folded strip while holding it in the center.

There are several methods of cutting out the pattern on the folded strip. Try the following, and then choose the method that works best for you.

A. Look at the pattern, and cut the strip freehand.

B. Look at the pattern, draw the design on the strip freehand, and then cut.

C. Trace the design, on lightweight paper, and cut this out. Place this pattern on the folded strip, and cut out the areas of the strip that are not covered.

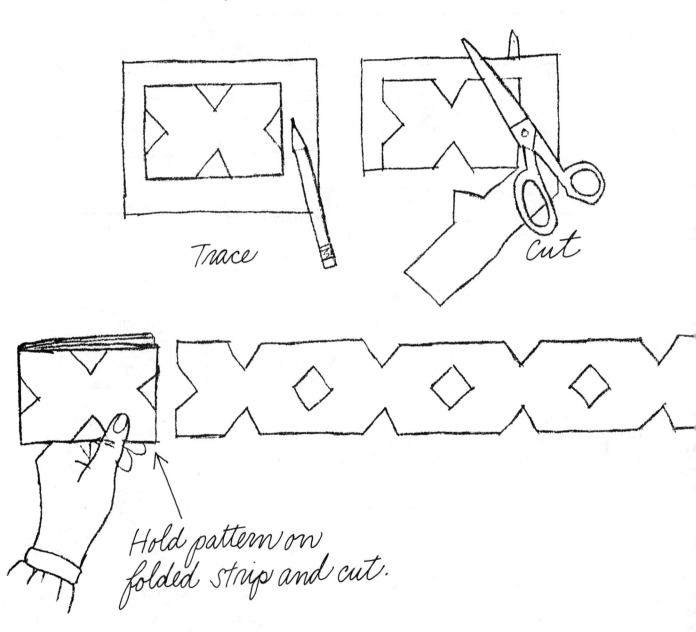

Trace

Cut

Hold pattern on folded strip and cut.

D. Trace the design on lightweight paper. Use carbon paper to transfer the design to lightweight cardboard. Cut out the pattern on the cardboard.

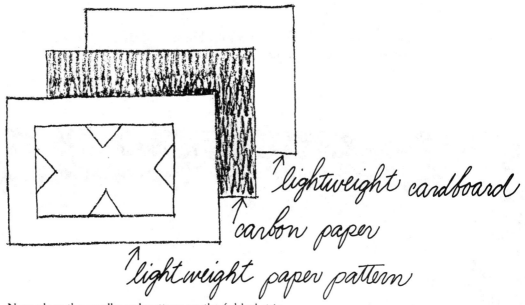

lightweight cardboard
carbon paper
lightweight paper pattern

Now place the cardboard pattern on the folded strip, and trace around it with a pencil. Cut along the lines you have drawn.

Open the folded strip, and cut as many more as you need to complete your border.

Step 6 Staple or pin the border strips around your bulletin board.

Using this six-step method, you are now ready to make any of the borders shown in this book. Once you are familiar with the technique, you might even want to create your own patterns.

Double borders can make very attractive bulletin boards. You can place the borders one inside the other, or you can overlap them.

Double Borders

General Borders

General Borders

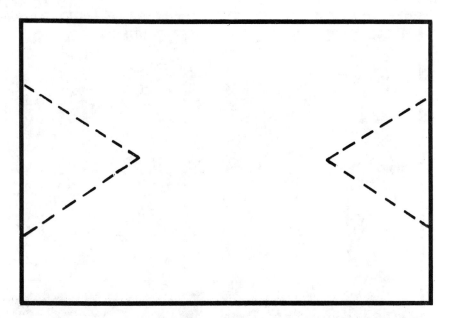

Plain Strip with Diamonds I

Plain Strip with Diamonds II

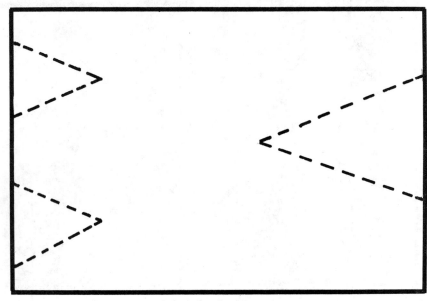

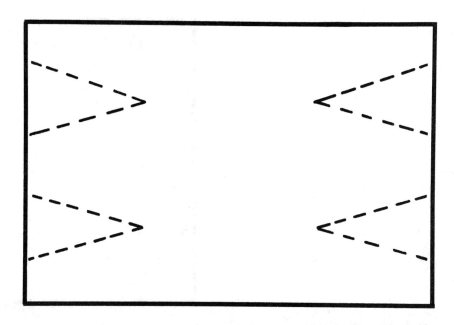

Plain Strip with Diamonds III

Circles and Ovals

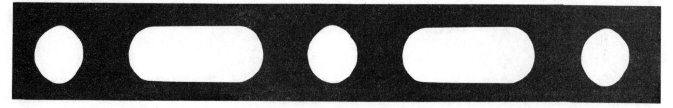

(See page 61 for double-size pattern.)

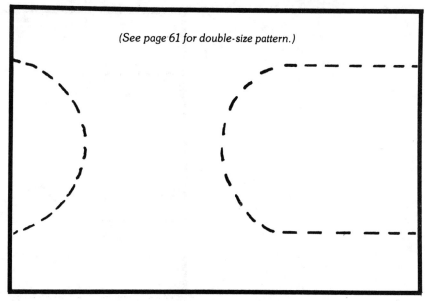

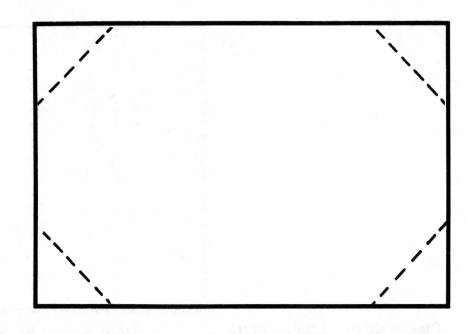

Solid Chain

Hollow Chain

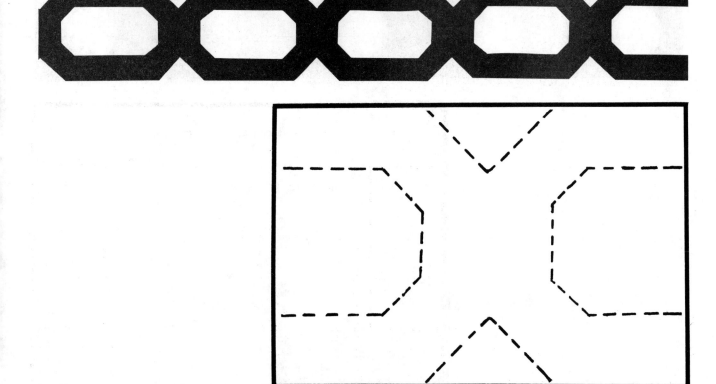

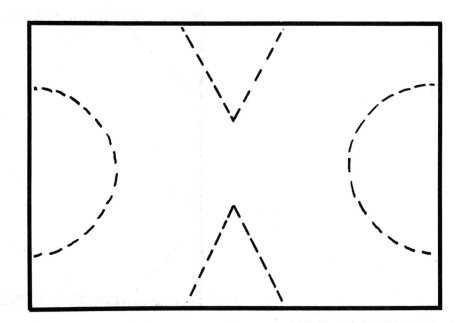

Chain with Circles

Chain with Squares

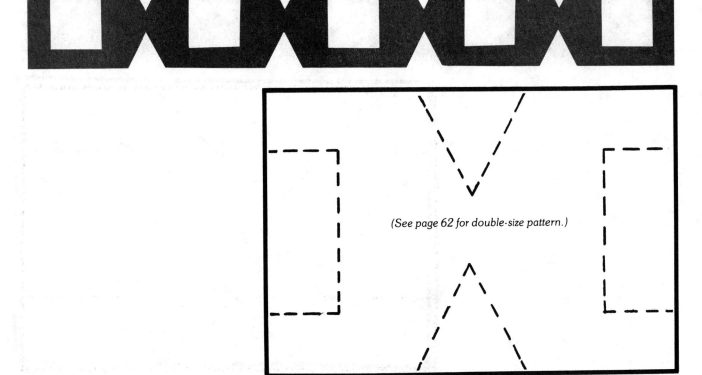

(See page 62 for double-size pattern.)

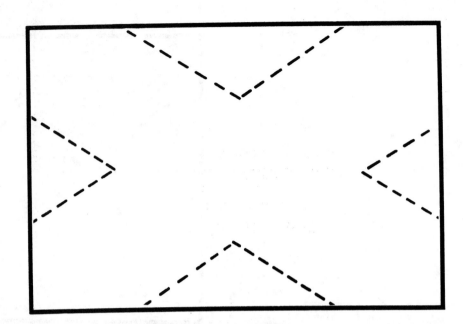

Chain with Diamonds I

Chain with Diamonds II

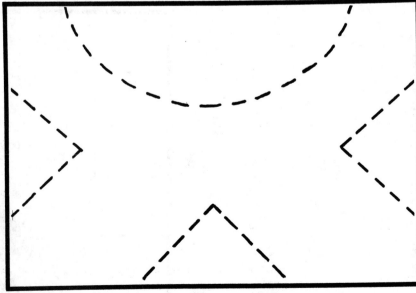

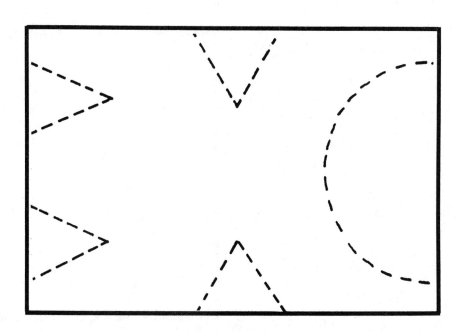

Circles and Diamonds

Diamonds and Squares

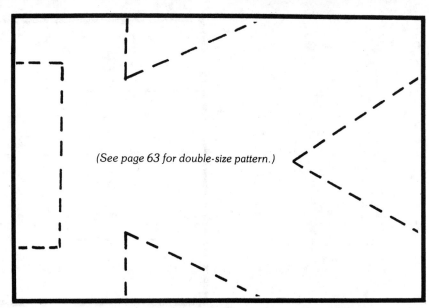

(See page 63 for double-size pattern.)

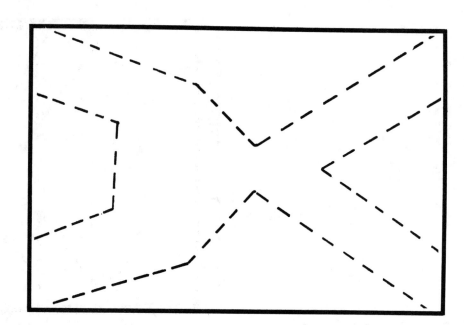

Diamonds and Hexagons

Hourglasses and Hexagons

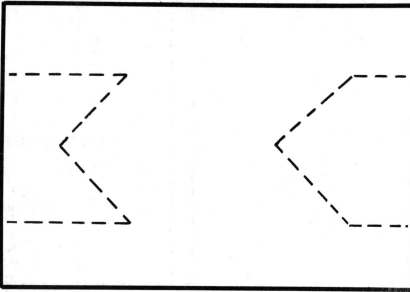

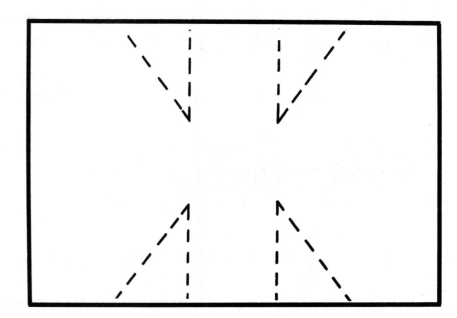

Bars and Octagons I

Bars and Octagons II

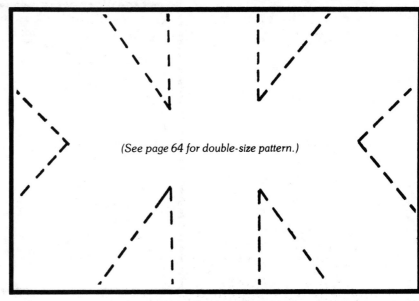

(See page 64 for double-size pattern.)

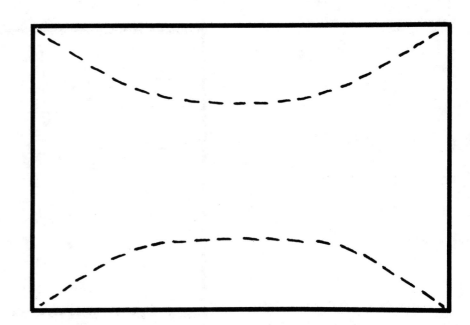

Scallops

Scallops and Peaks

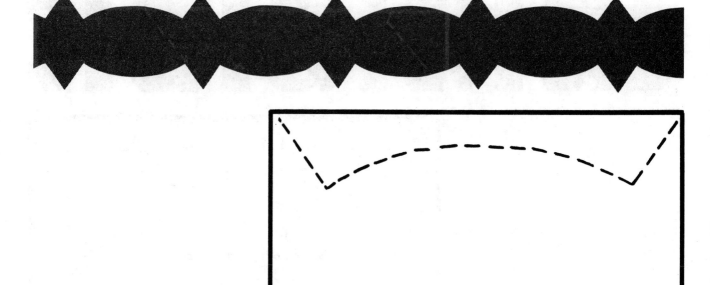

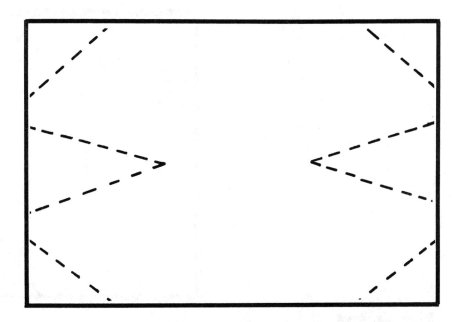

Flat Diamonds I

Flat Diamonds II

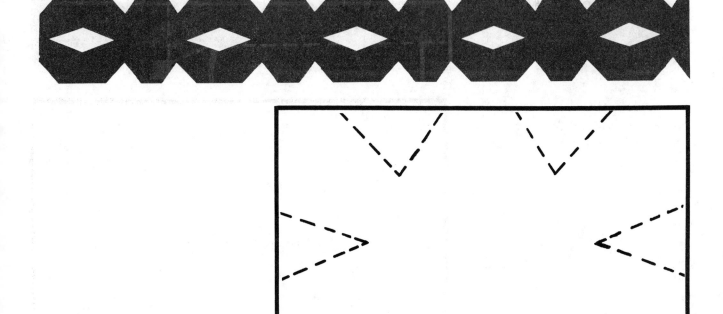

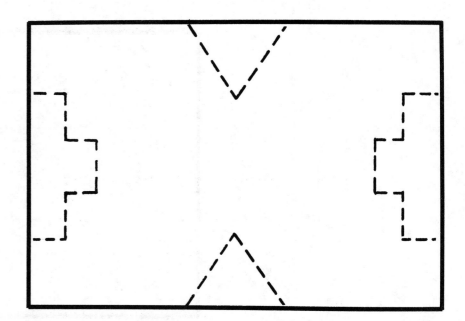

Plain Crosses

Fancy Crosses

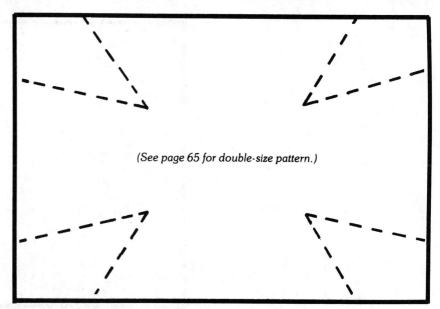

(See page 65 for double-size pattern.)

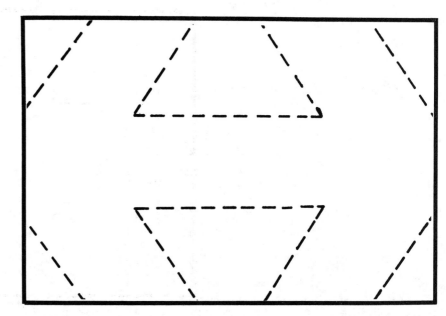

X's

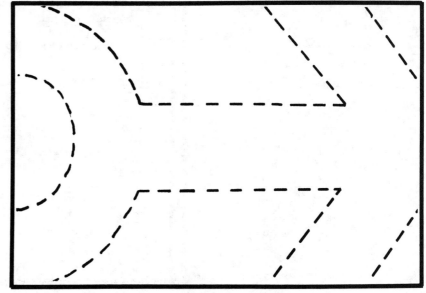

X's and O's

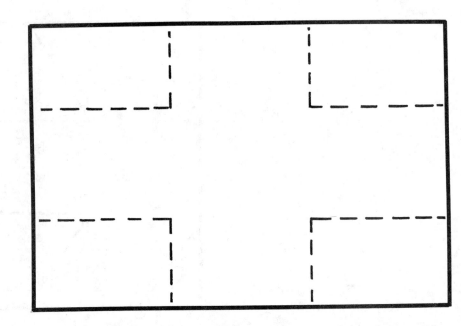

Fence

Bridges and Towers

(See page 66 for double-size pattern.)

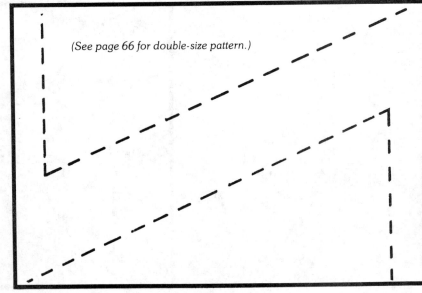

Fall Borders

Fall Motifs

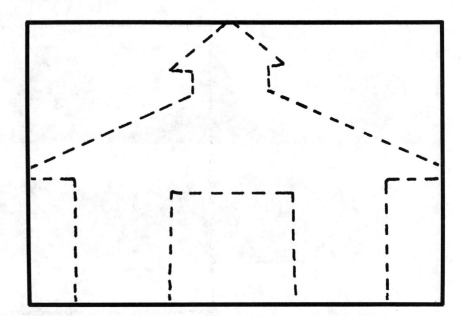

Schoolhouses

Schoolhouses and Apples

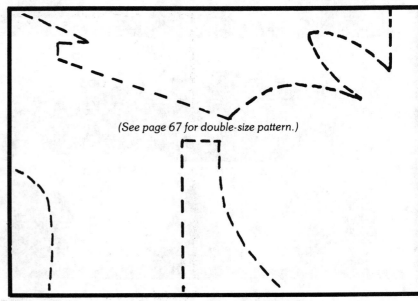

(See page 67 for double-size pattern.)

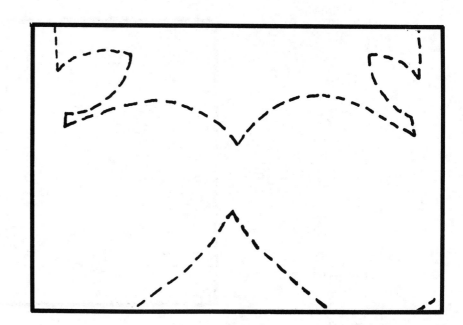

Apples

Students

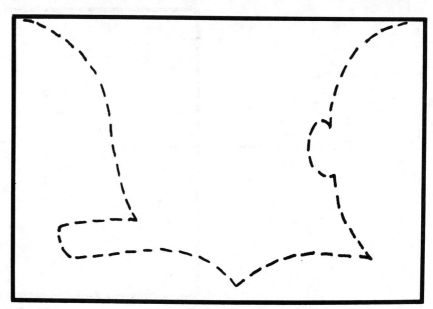

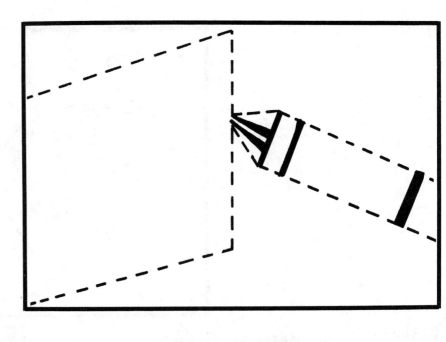

Draw in lines on crayons.

Crayons and Books

Pencils and Papers

Add headings to papers.

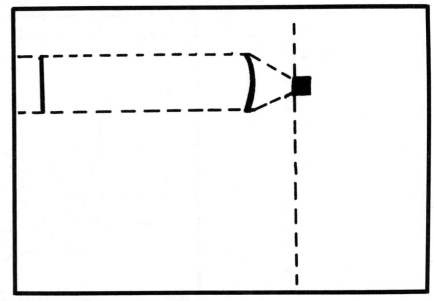

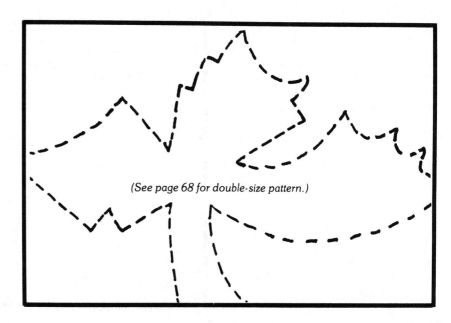

(See page 68 for double-size pattern.)

Fall Leaves I

Fall Leaves II

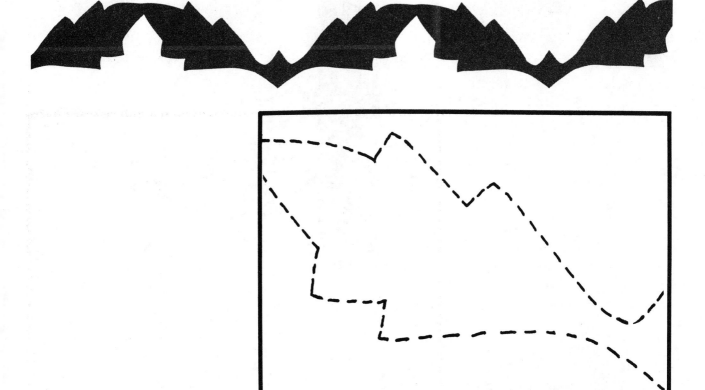

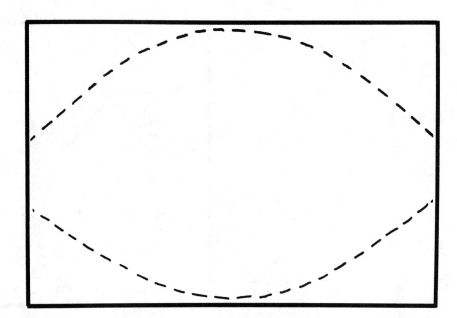

Footballs

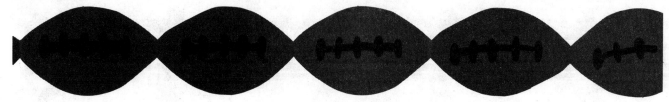

Either cut out laces and paste them
on footballs, or draw them in.

Pattern for laces

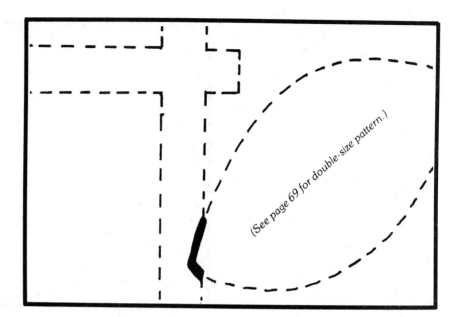

(See page 69 for double-size pattern.)

Footballs and Goalposts

Add lines to define footballs.
Either cut and paste on laces,
or draw them in.

Pattern for laces

Fall Holidays

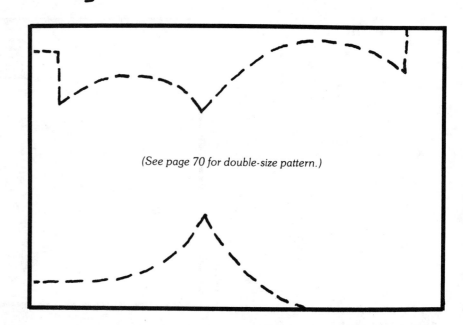

(See page 70 for double-size pattern.)

Jack-o'-Lanterns

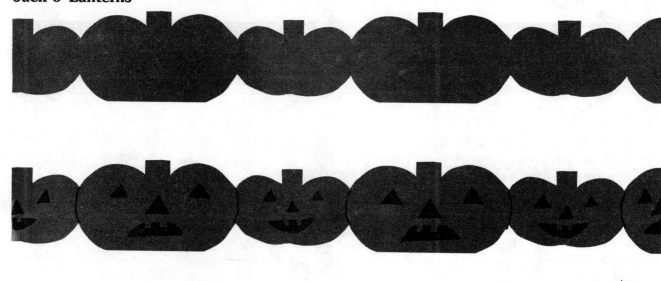

Cut and paste features on jack-o'-lanterns.
Add lines to separate jack-o'-lanterns.

Patterns for jack-o'-lantern faces

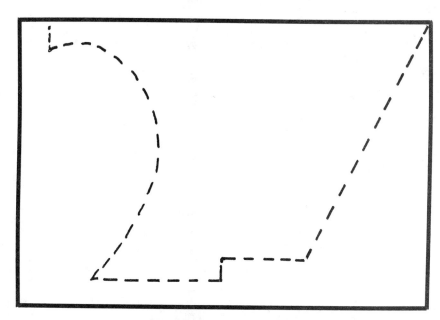

Witches' Hats and Jack-o'-Lanterns

Add lines as shown.
Cut and paste parts on border.

BROWN

YELLOW

Patterns for jack-o'-lantern faces

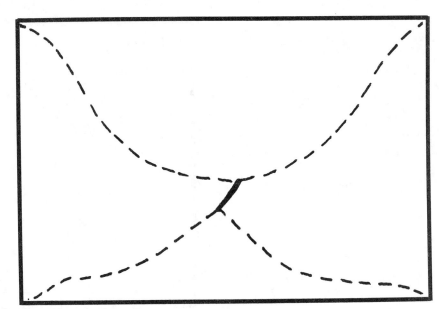

Add lines to separate ghosts.
Add dots for eyes.

Ghosts

Bats

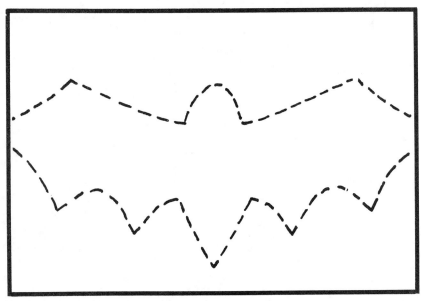

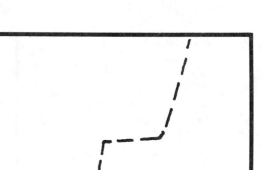
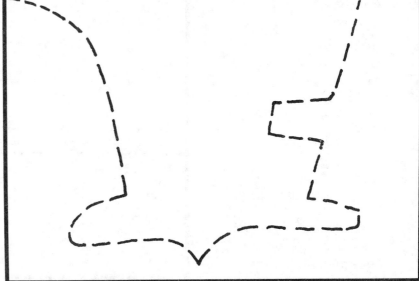

Pilgrims

Native Americans

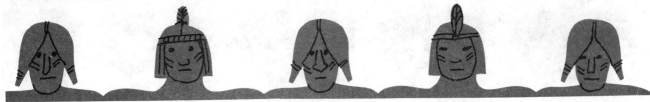

Students can draw in faces for the Pilgrims and Native Americans.

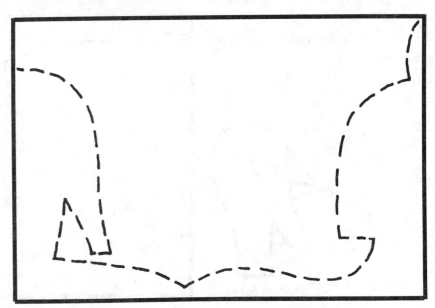

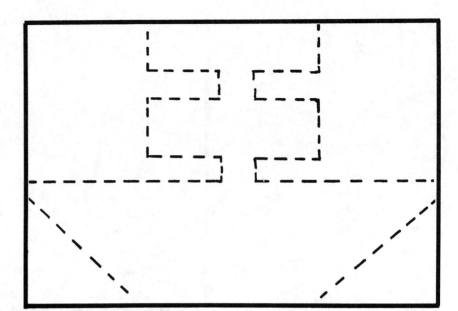

Mayflower

Turkeys

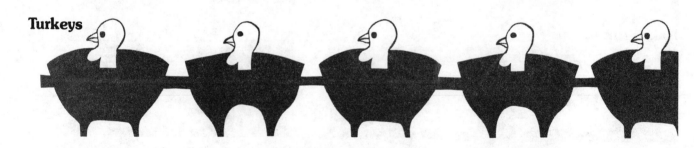

Cut and paste heads onto turkeys.

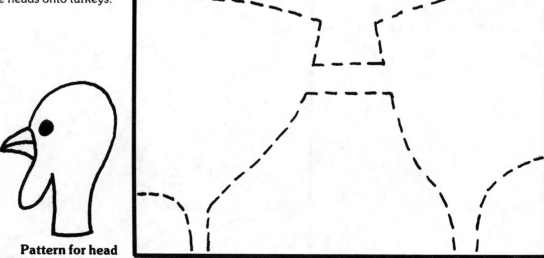

Pattern for head

Winter Borders

Winter Motifs

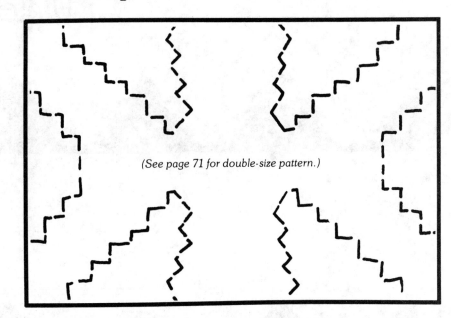

(See page 71 for double-size pattern.)

Snowflakes

Snowballs and Snowflakes

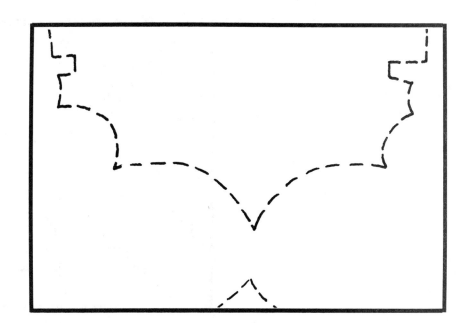

Snowmen

Snowcapped Mountains

Add snow to mountaintops.

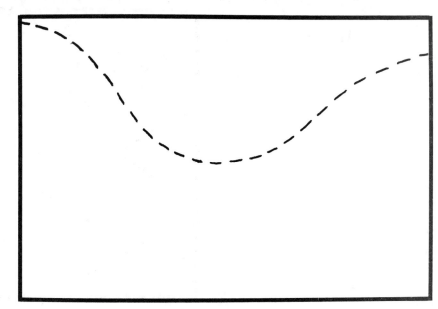

Winter Holidays

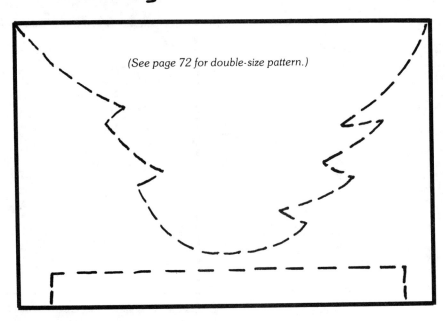

(See page 72 for double-size pattern.)

Christmas Trees

Ornaments

You may wish to draw designs on the ornaments.

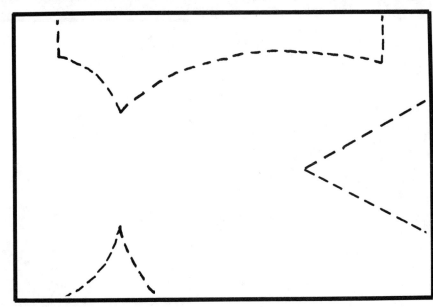

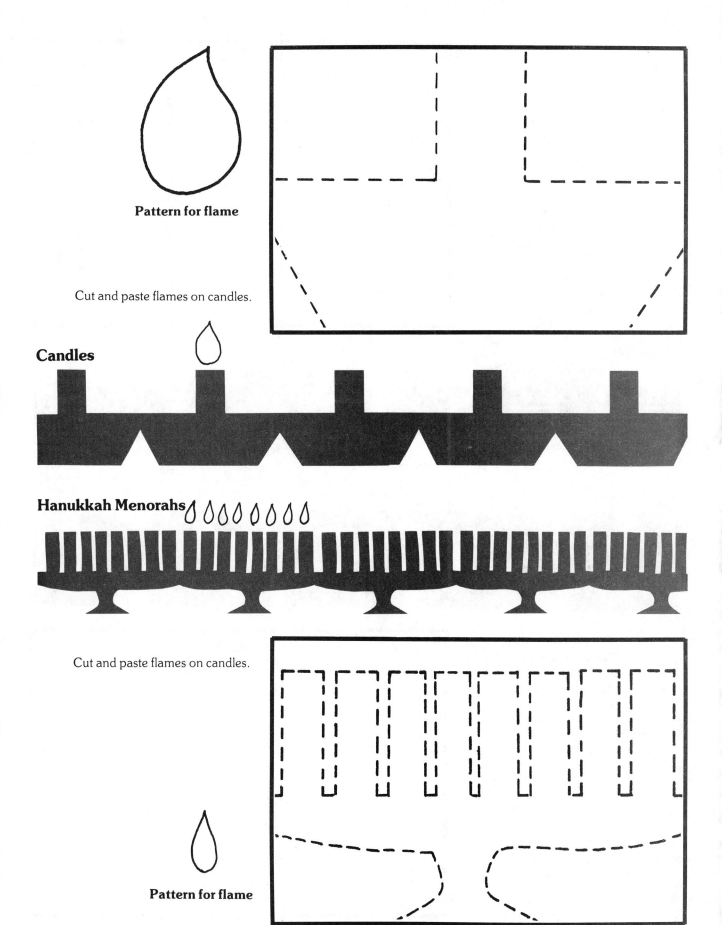

Pattern for flame

Cut and paste flames on candles.

Candles

Hanukkah Menorahs

Cut and paste flames on candles.

Pattern for flame

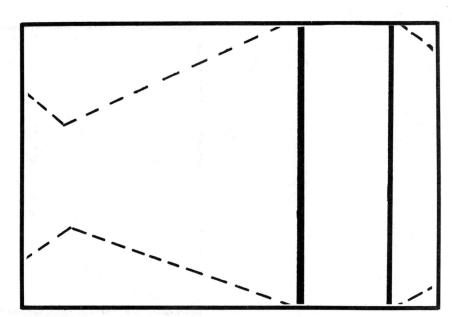

Add lines and dates
with crayon or felt-tip pen.

Megaphones

Date Border

Cut out numbers,
and paste them on the border.

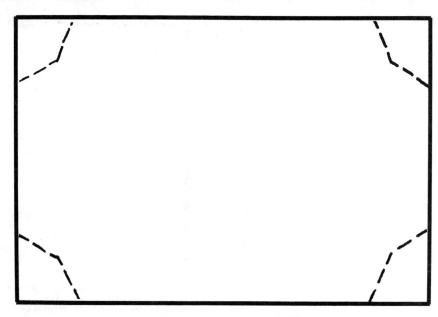

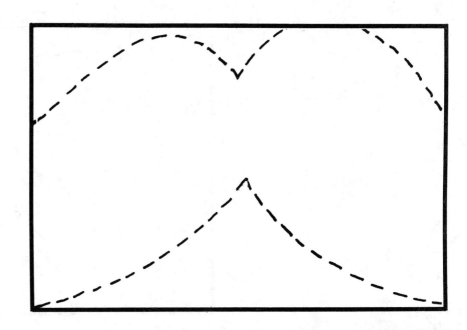

Solid Hearts

Ring in the New Year

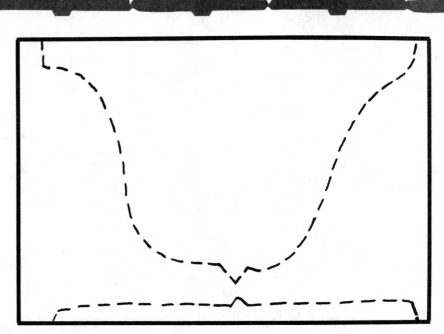

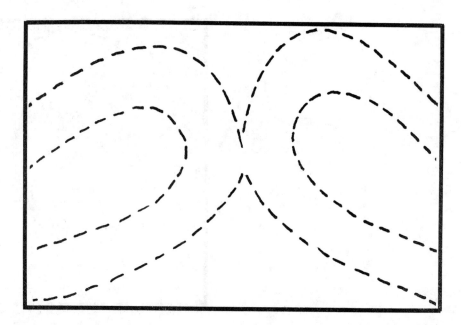

Hollow Hearts

Hearts of All Sizes

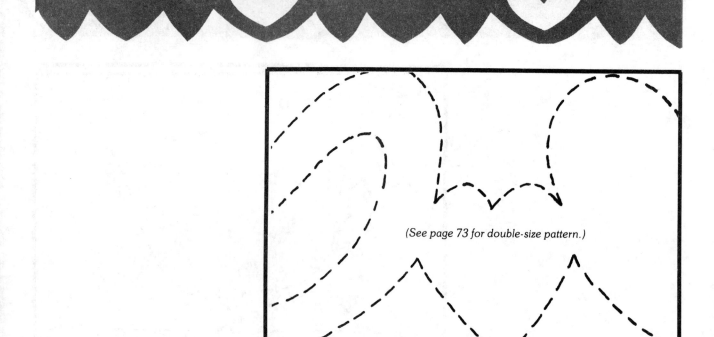

(See page 73 for double-size pattern.)

Instant Borders copyright © 1979

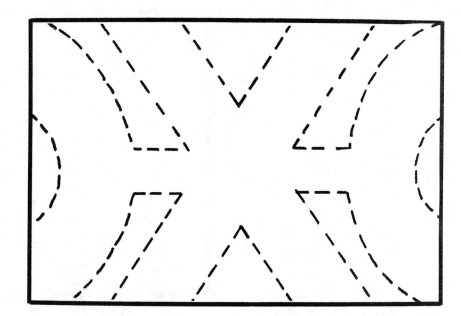

Hugs and Kisses

Plain Border with Small Hearts

Cut and paste hearts on border.

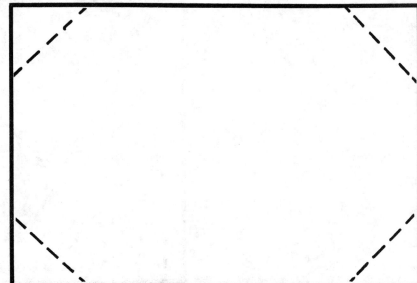

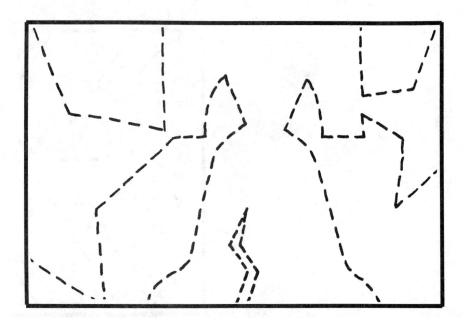

Liberty Bell and Stars

Lincoln and Washington

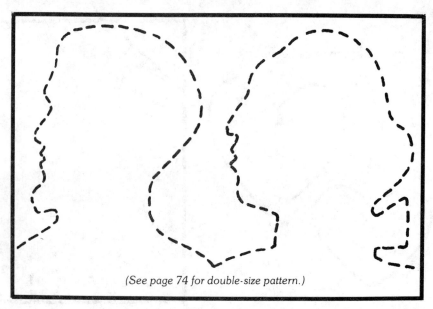

(See page 74 for double-size pattern.)

Spring Borders

Spring Motifs

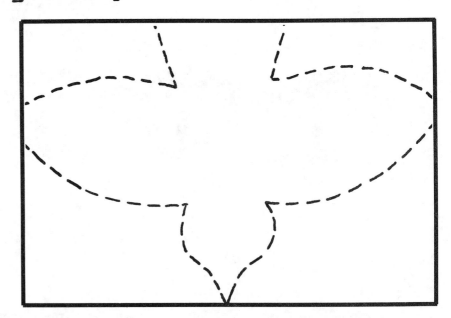

Bluebirds

Baby Birds

Draw lines as shown, and draw in eyes.

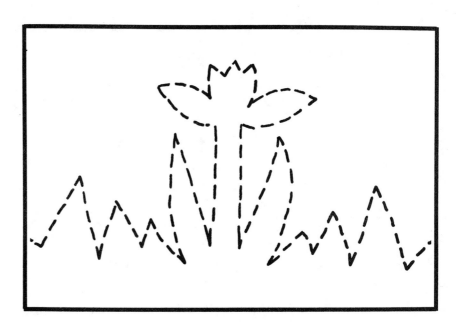

Daffodils and Grass

Kites

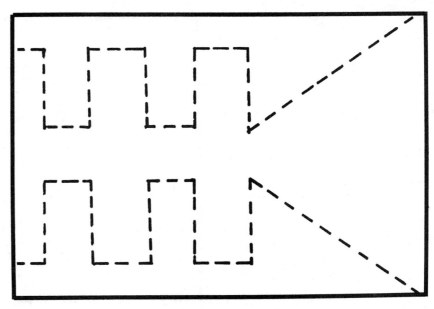

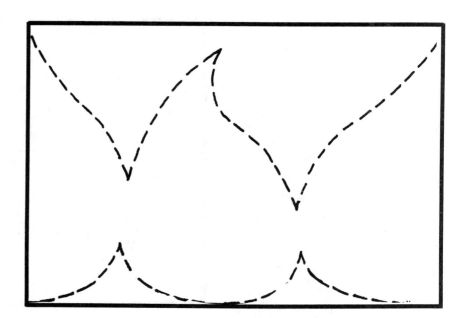

Raindrops

Umbrellas

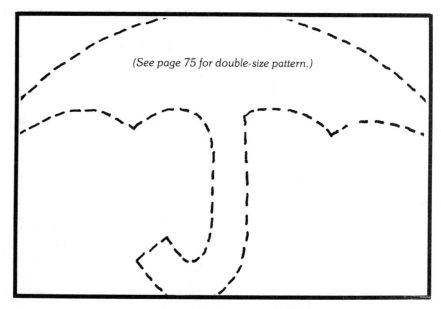

(See page 75 for double-size pattern.)

Instant Borders copyright © 1979

Pattern for centers
Cut and paste centers into flowers.

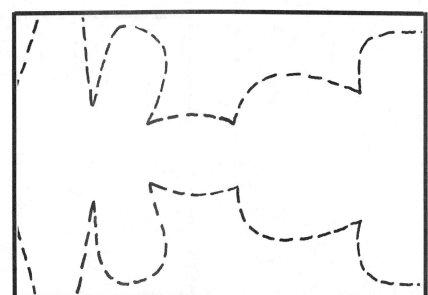

Spring Flowers I

Spring Flowers II

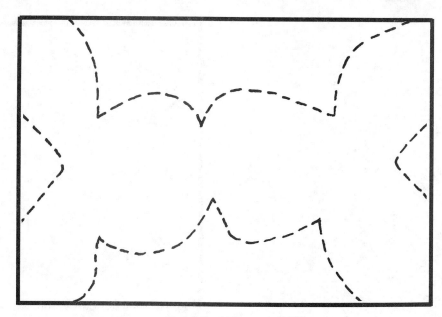

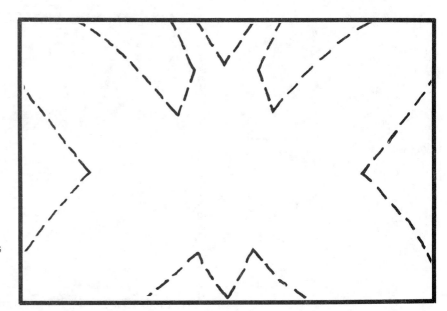

You may wish to draw designs on the butterflies' wings.

Butterflies

Butterflies and Flowers

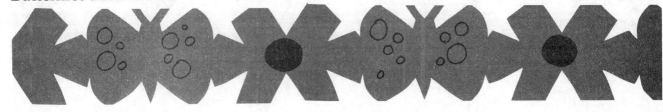

Cut-and-paste centers can be added to the flowers.

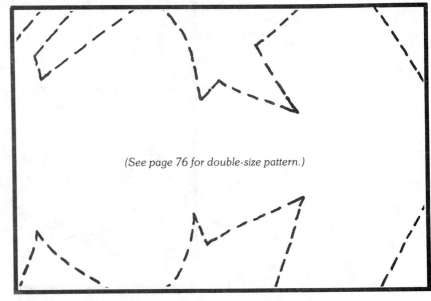

(See page 76 for double-size pattern.)

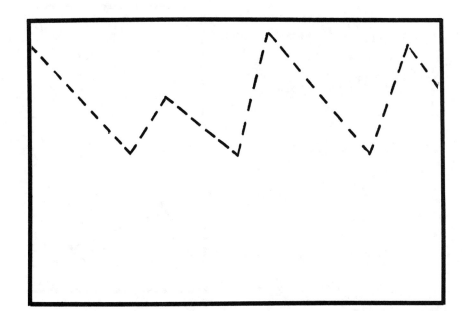

Grass

Flowerpots

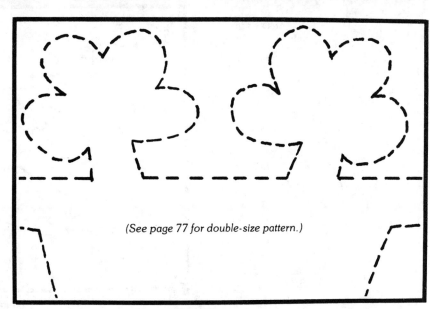

(See page 77 for double-size pattern.)

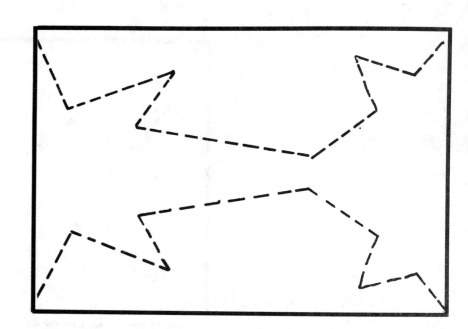

Bright Stars

Suns

Add lines as shown.

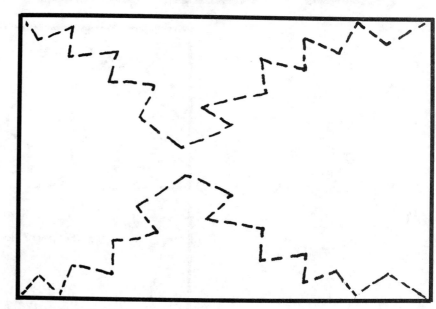

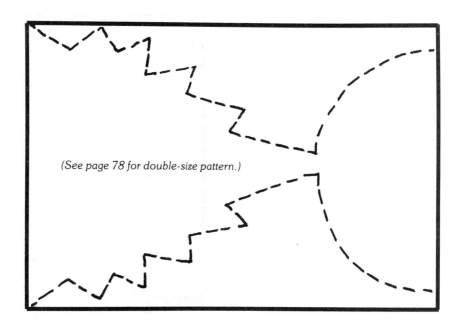

(See page 78 for double-size pattern.)

Draw happy faces in the circles.

Suns and Happy Faces

Balls and Bats

Add lines as shown.

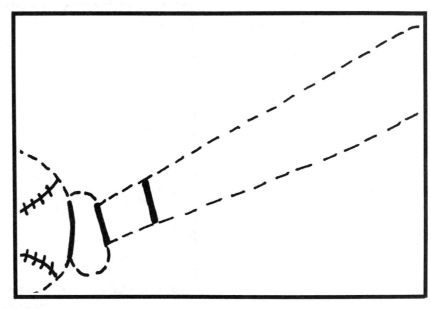

Spring Holidays

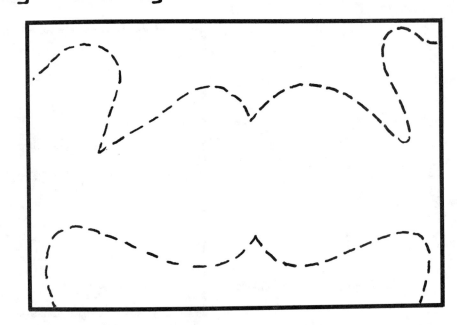

Shamrocks

May Baskets and Flowers

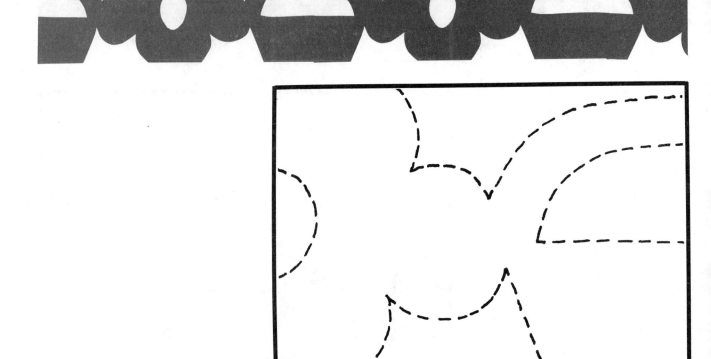

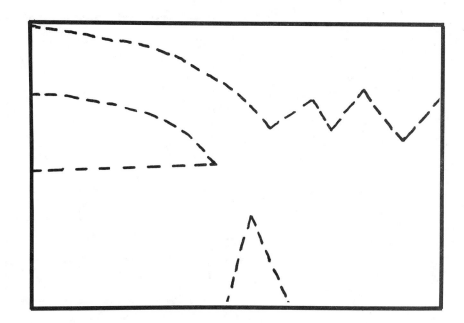

Baskets and Grass

Easter Eggs

Let children decorate the eggs
with crayon or felt-tip pen.

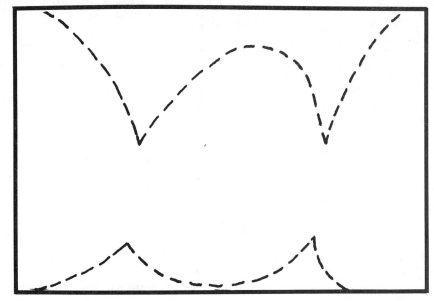

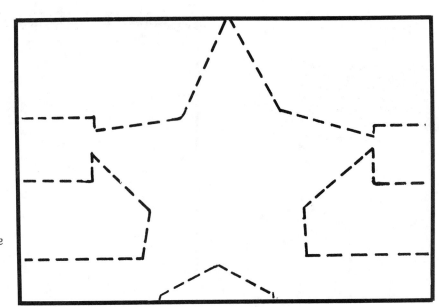

Make this border white, and place it on a red background.

Stars and Stripes

Frames

The students can draw small pictures representing their plans for the summer. The pictures can be pasted behind the frames.

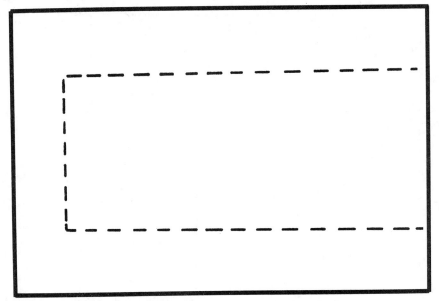

International Borders

International Borders

Pattern

Cut and paste on dots for eyes.

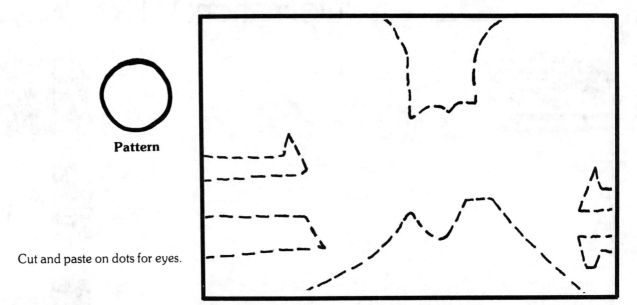

African Masks

Maracas

Students can decorate the maracas.

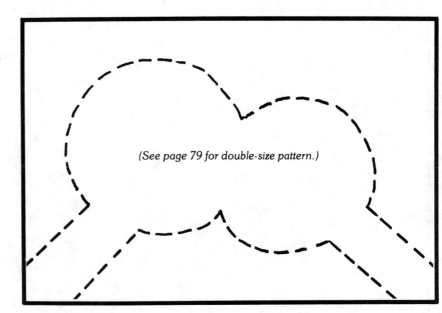

(See page 79 for double-size pattern.)

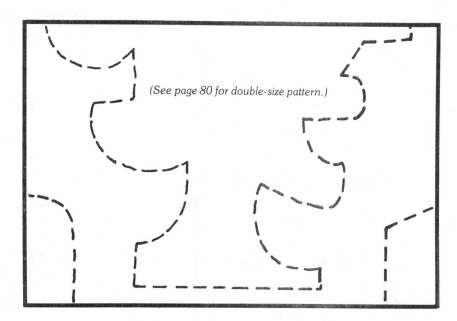

(See page 80 for double-size pattern.)

Pagodas

Flags of Many Countries

Students can draw in
details of the flags.

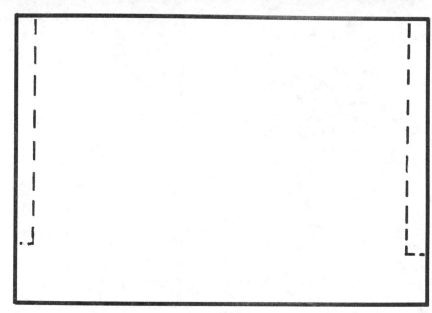

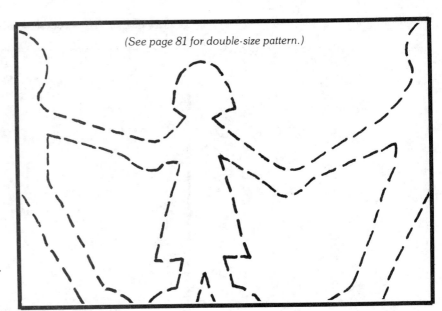

(See page 81 for double-size pattern.)

The students can add faces and costumes with felt-tip pens or crayons.

Children from Many Lands I

Children from Many Lands II

Note: The frame border on page 54 can be used for any special study on an international theme. For example, the students could draw pictures of important men and women from a particular nation or ethnic group.

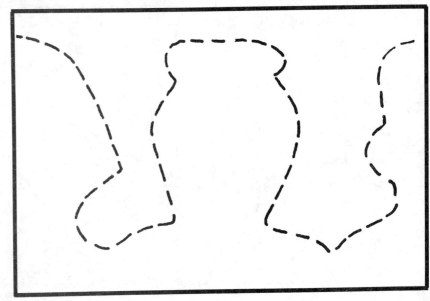

Appendix

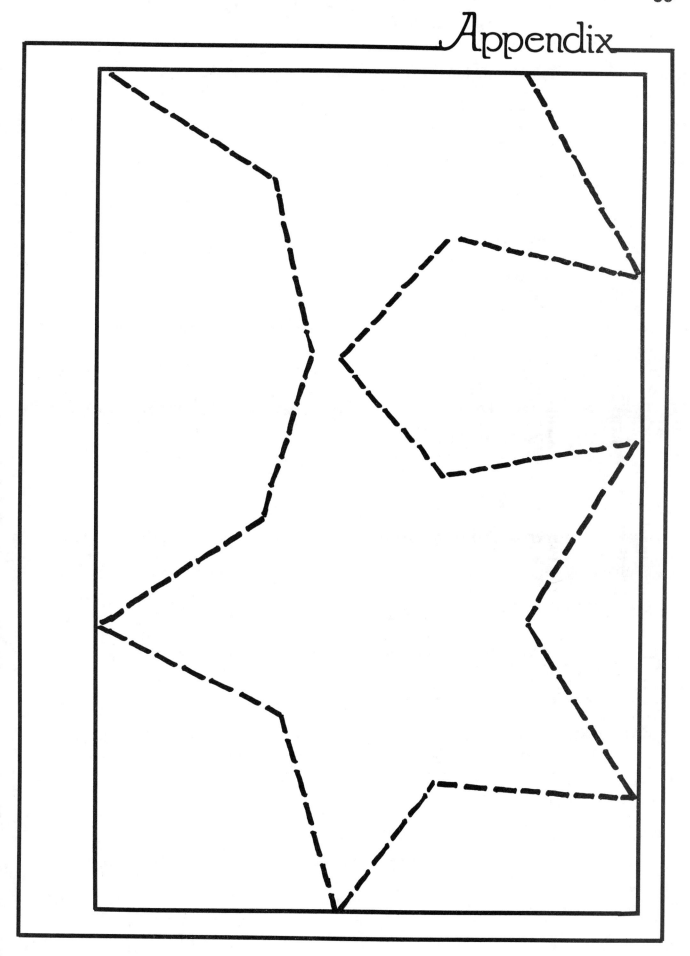

Double-Size Borders

Patterns included in this section are:

The scaled-up patterns in this section may be used to create borders for larger displays. To use them, cut *two* strips of construction paper 18 inches by 6 inches, and fold each in half. Slide one piece inside the other, folded ends together. Then place the double-size pattern over the folded strips, and cut as with the regular-size patterns.

Circles and Ovals

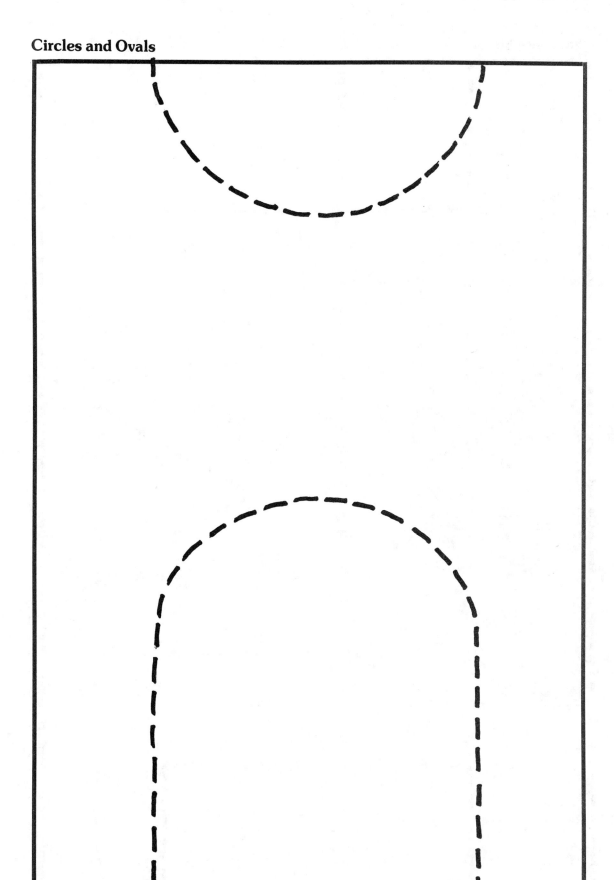

Instant Borders copyright © 1979

Chain with Squares

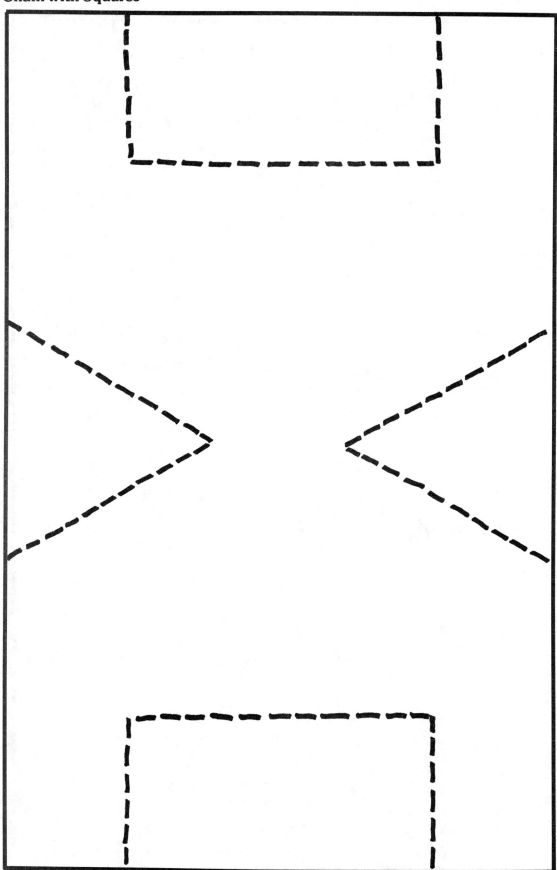

Diamonds and Squares

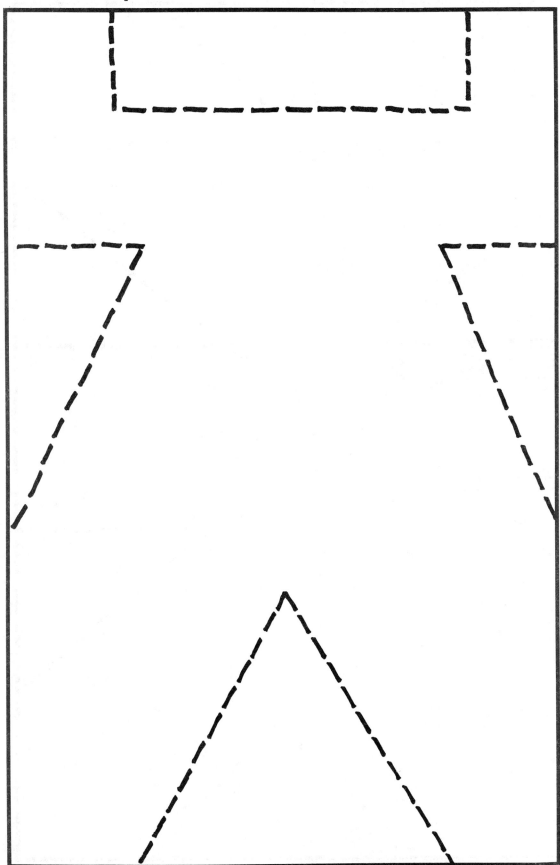

Bars and Octagons II

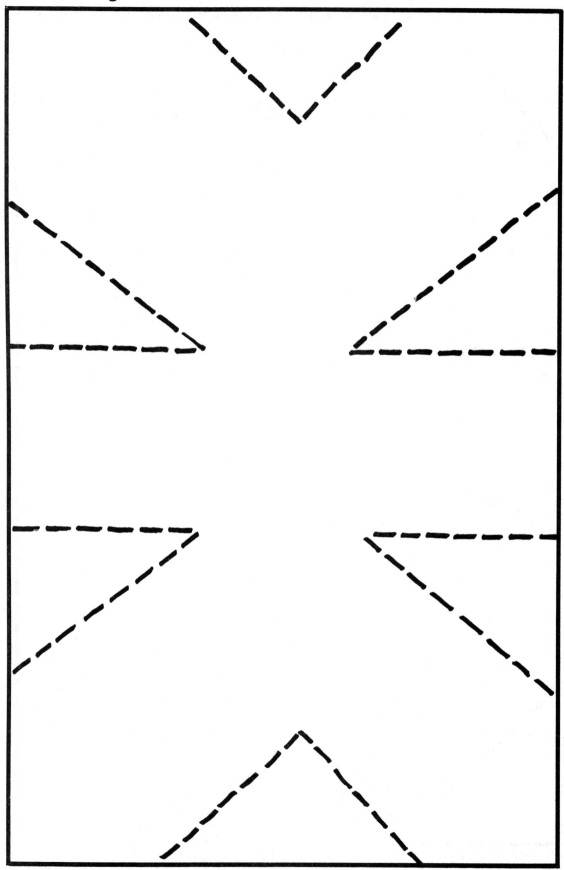

Fancy Crosses

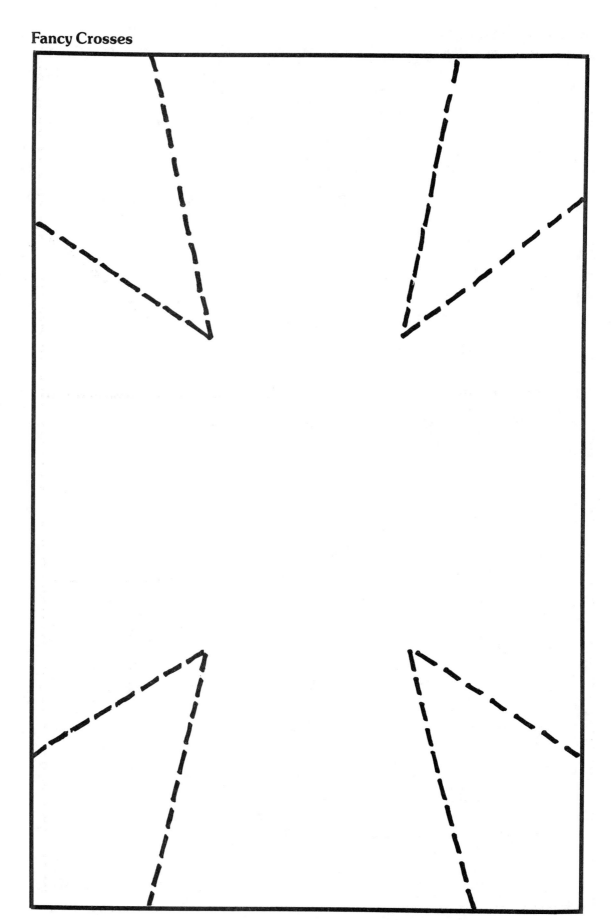

Bridges and Towers

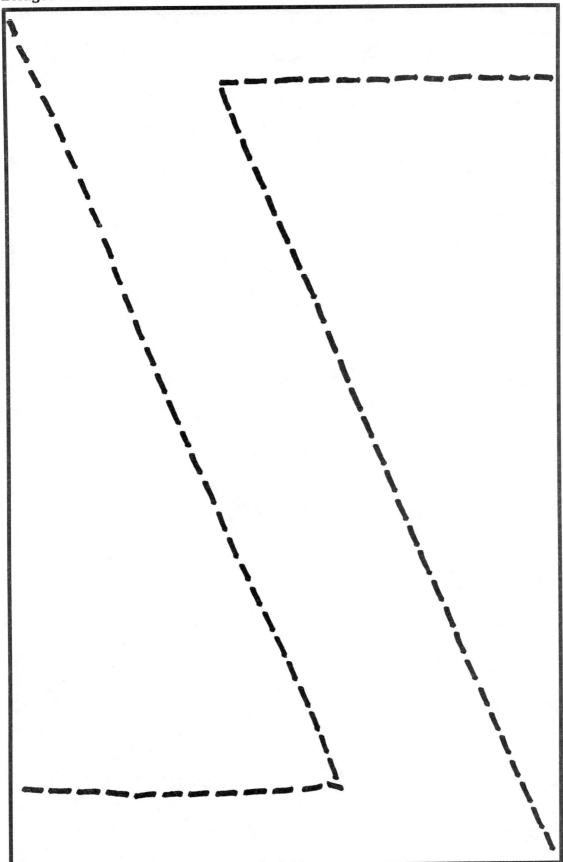

Schoolhouses and Apples

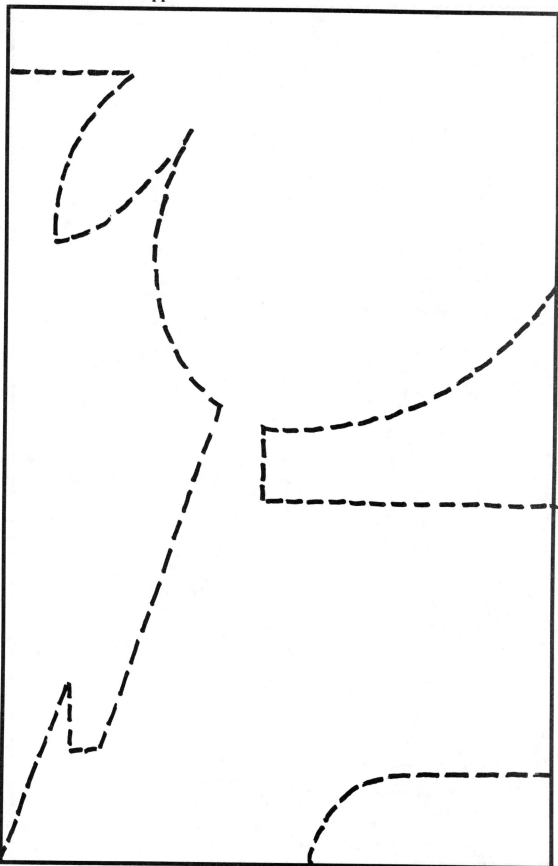

Fall Leaves

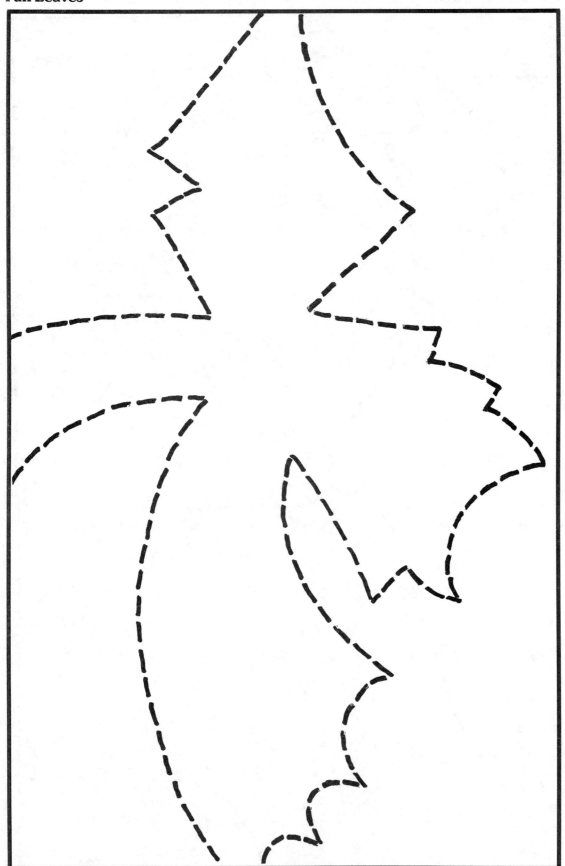

Footballs and Goalposts

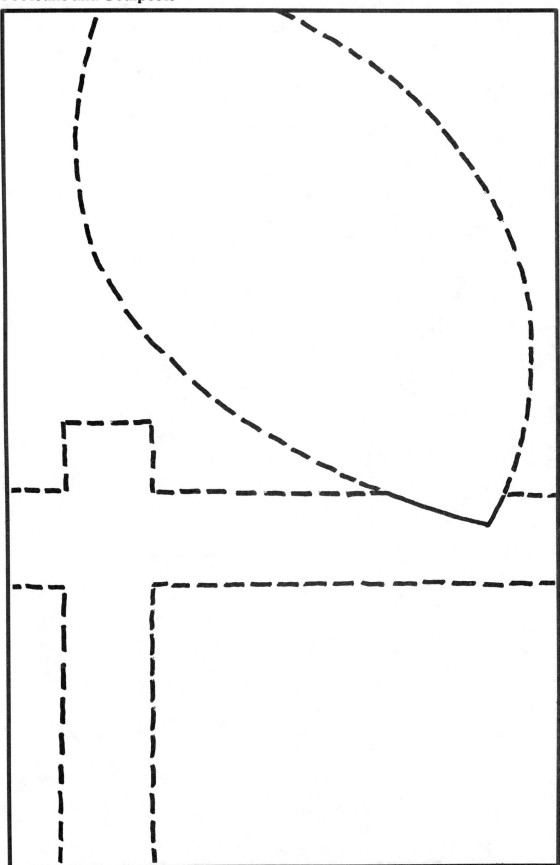

Jack-o'-Lanterns

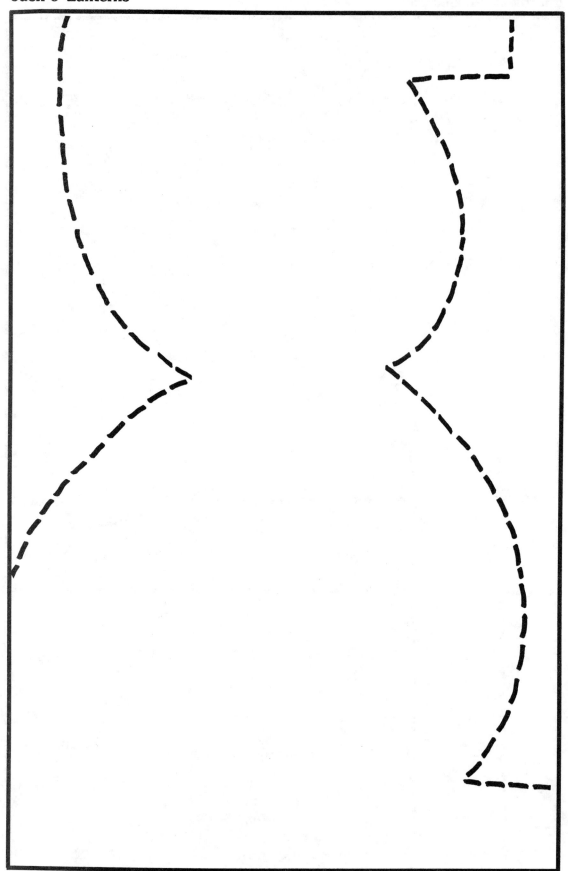

Snowflakes

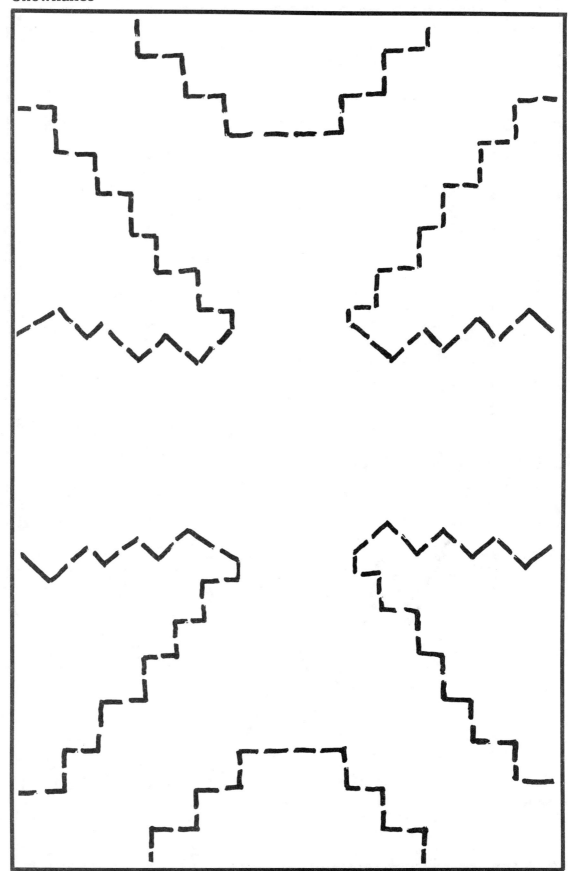

Christmas Trees

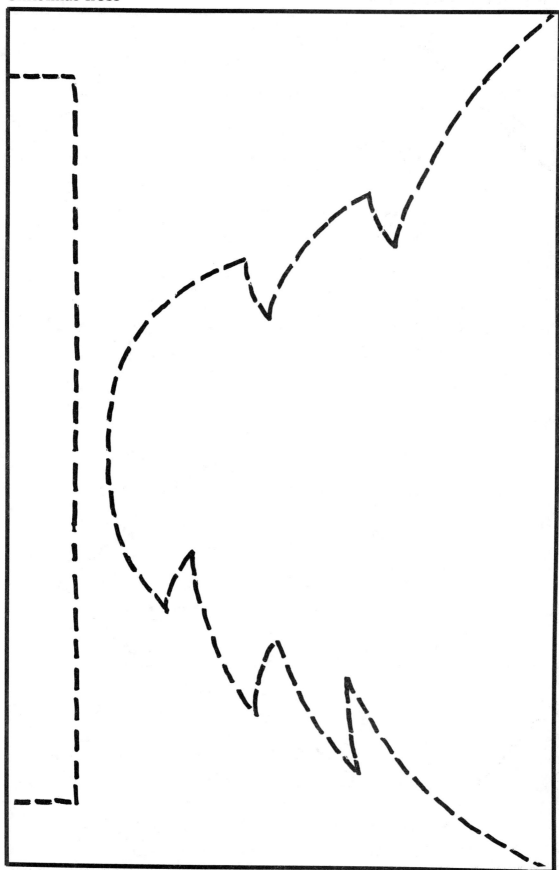

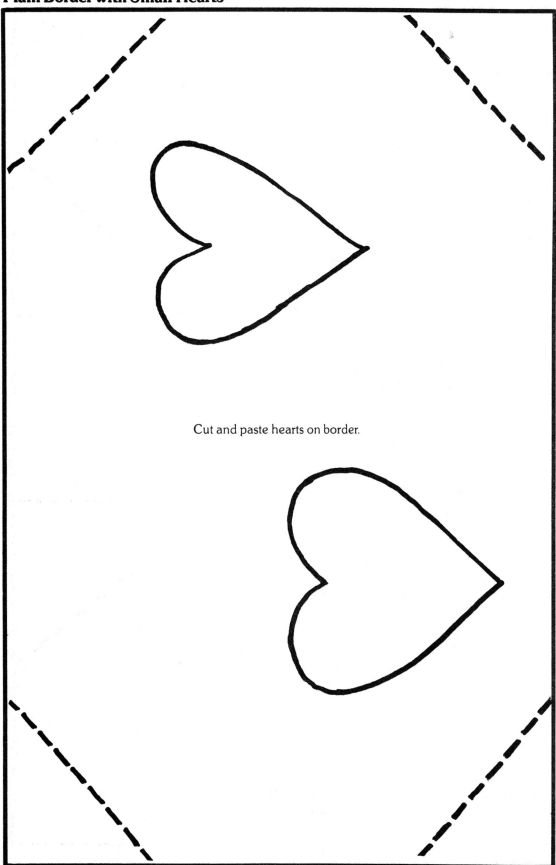

Plain Border with Small Hearts

Cut and paste hearts on border.

Lincoln and Washington

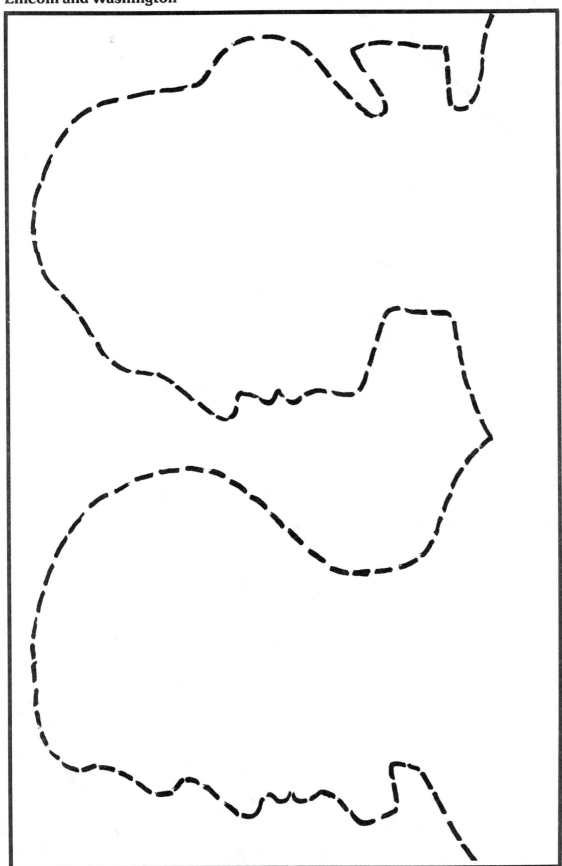

Umbrellas

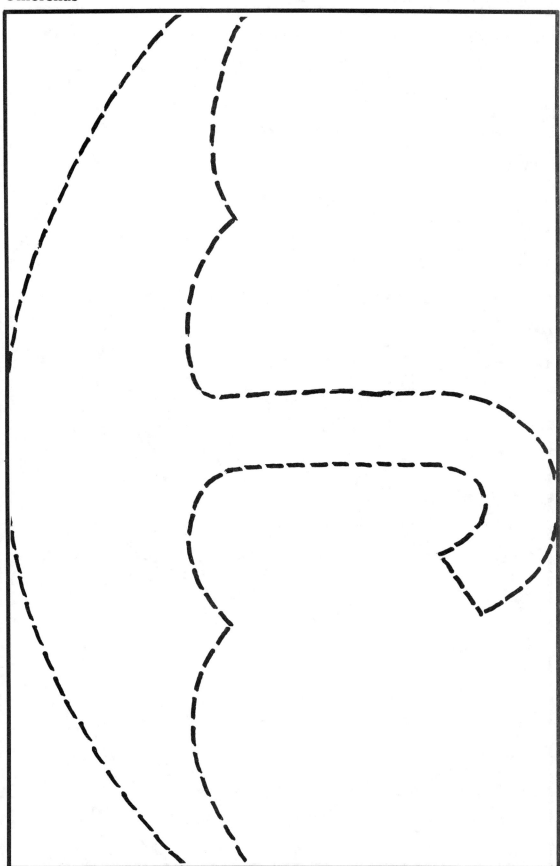

Butterflies and Flowers

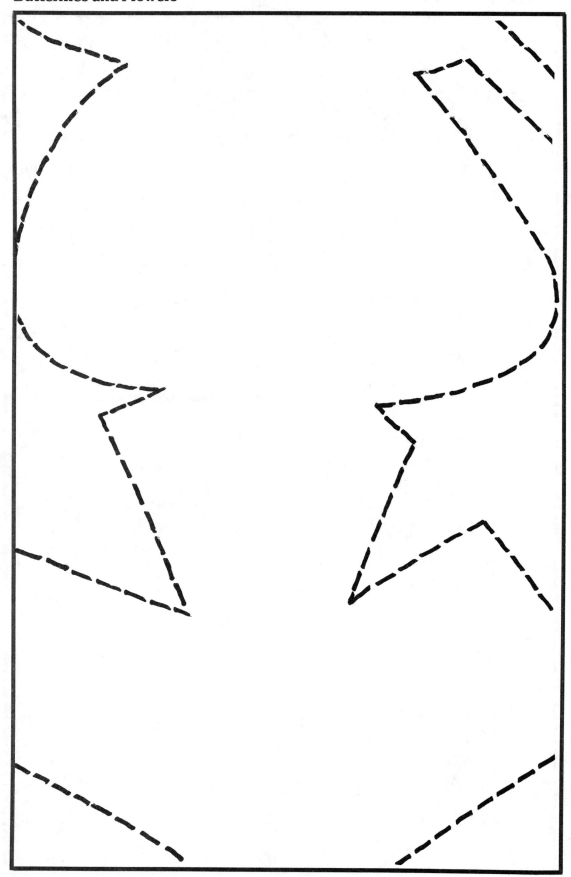

Flowerpots

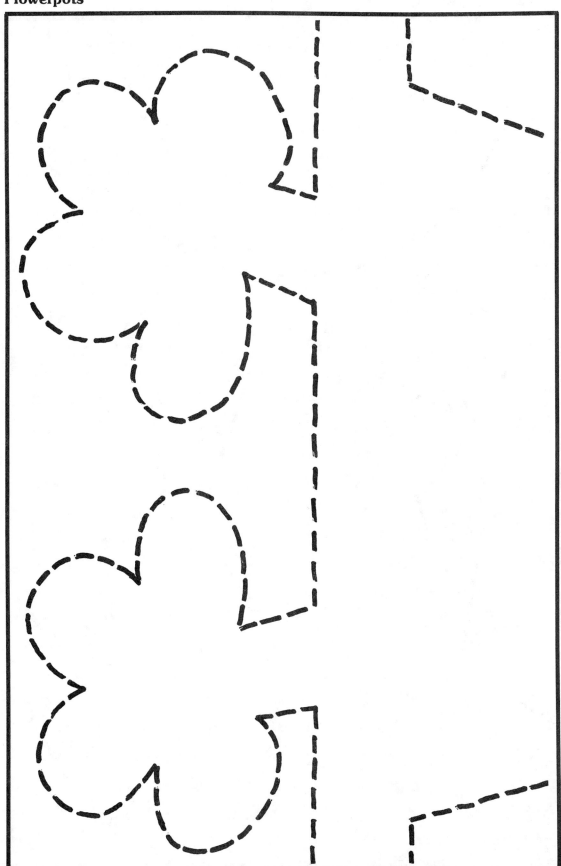

Sun and Happy Faces

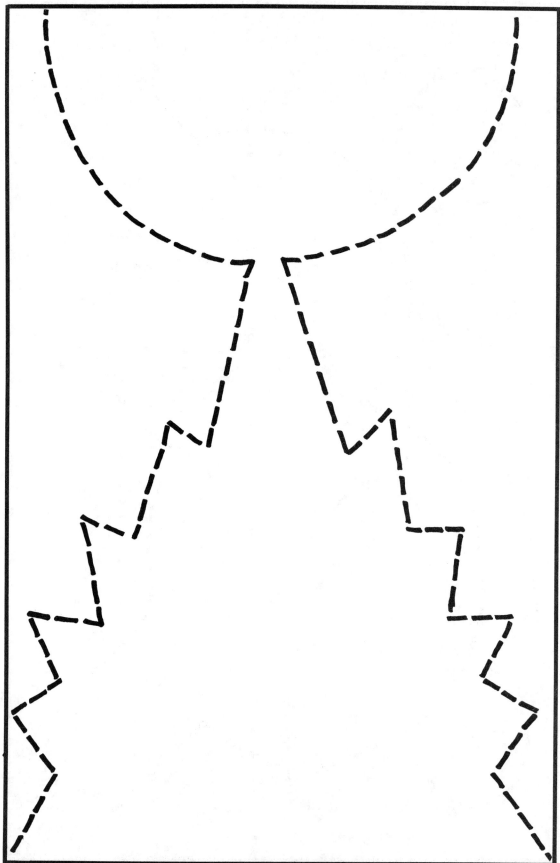

Maracas

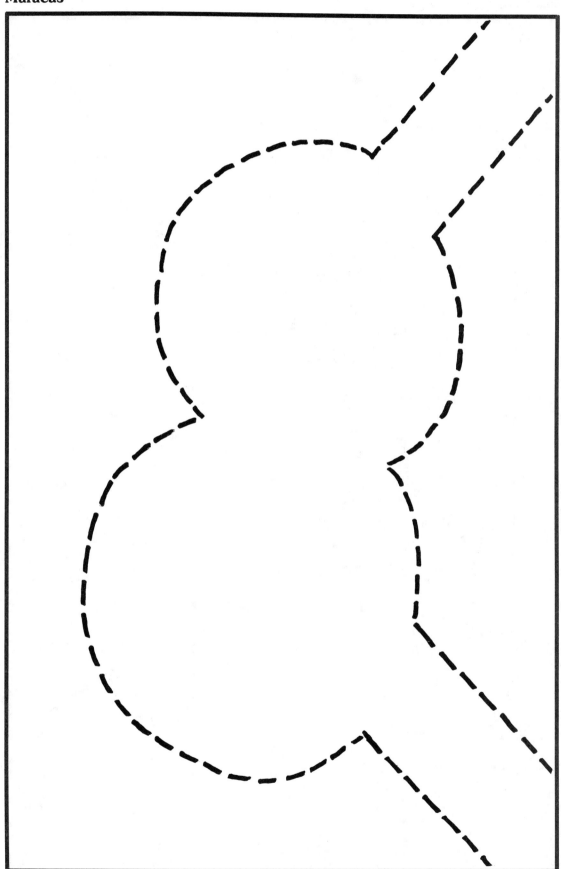

Pagodas

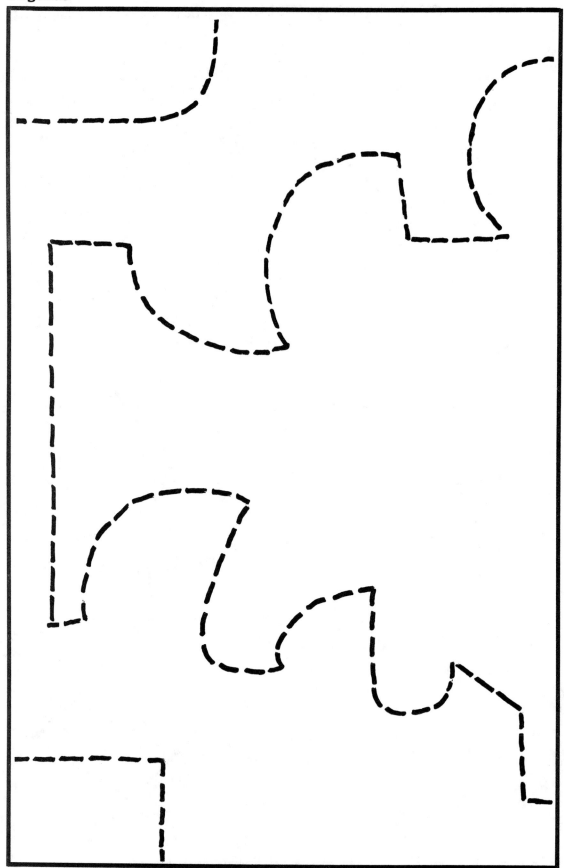

Children from Many Lands

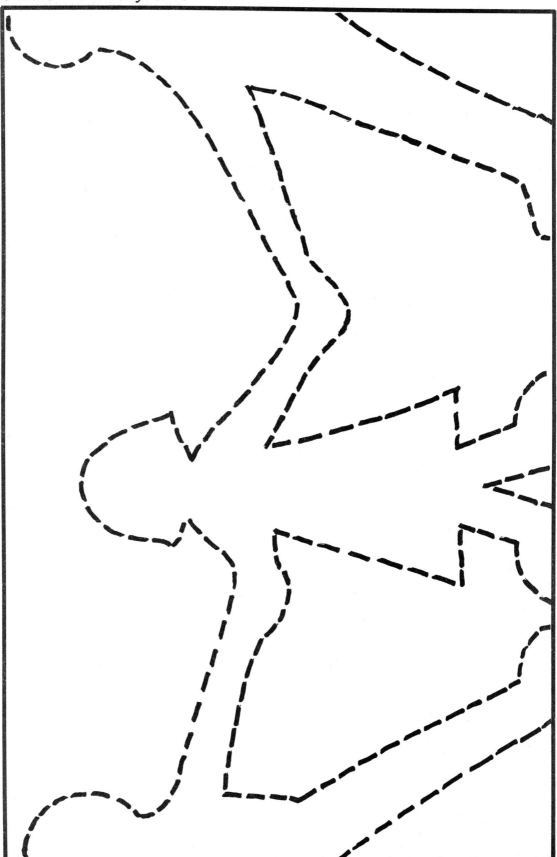

Fearon Teacher Aids
The Books That Free You to Teach

Additional titles to help you create effective
bulletin boards and educational materials:

AWARDS, REWARDS, AND MARVELOUS MESSAGES: The best collection of awards and rewards ever assembled. Seasonal awards, pictures to color and take home, award games and puzzles, "helper" awards, and messages for parents. You'll always have just the right aid to motivate, reinforce, or improve student performance. #0535

HOLIDAYS FOR THE BASICS—Math and Science: A time-saving collection of illustrated activities. Worksheets, board games, and file folder games with clear directions for use give you the chance to add your own skills materials. Perfect for tailoring materials to your class needs. #3698

HOLIDAYS FOR THE BASICS—Language Arts and Social Studies: A super set of holiday themes coupled with worksheets, board games, and file folder games gives you the opportunity to add your skills materials for individualizing activities. Charming illustrations will motivate students' work. #3699

SHAPE-A-STORY Reproducible Story Shapes and Ideas for Creative Writing Booklets: Writing skills grow with these super story-starter ideas, bulletin board layouts, and reproducible story shapes—with both writing lines and covers to illustrate. #6392

SHAPE-A-POEM Reproducible Shapes and Ideas for Creative Poetry Booklets: All students will enjoy writing poetry with these delightful booklet projects. Each lesson has a poetic device to teach, a poem shape to reproduce—with both writing lines and covers to illustrate—as well as bulletin board layouts and teaching ideas. #6393

SHAPE-A-SOUND Reproducible Story Shapes for Phonics Practice and Creative Writing: Each phonics-focused activity has a story starter and a coordinated writing shape. There is a helpful word list in the teacher's guide. Students get writing practice and phonics reinforcement. #6394

BASIC BORDERS Easy-to-Make Subject Area Borders That Help You Teach: Kids will enjoy cutting, pasting, coloring, and adding their own touches to borders with health, math, language arts, science, music, reading, social studies, and p.e. themes. #2144

THE BIG FEARON BULLETIN BOARD BOOK: More than 600 project-a-pattern ideas in 23 subject areas. Create hundreds of imaginative, educational bulletin boards and variations using these visual elements. #0702